The Way to the Happiness of Peace

Understanding the Basics of Insight Meditation

Sayadaw U Pandita

Compiled by
Sujiva

Buddhist Publication Society
Kandy • Sri Lanka

Published in 2001

Buddhist Publication Society
P.O. Box 61
54, Sangharaja Mawatha
Kandy, Sri Lanka

Originally published by Inward Path Publisher, 1997.
Issued in the Wheel Series with the consent of the original publisher.

National Library of Sri Lanka –
Cataloguing–in–Publication Data

Pandita himi, Sayadaw U

The way to the happiness of peace : understanding the basics of insight meditation / Sayadaw U. Pandita himi - Kandy : Buddhist Publication Society - 2001
48p.; 18.5cm.

ISBN 955–24–0220-4

i. 294.34435 DDC 21 ii. Title

1. Meditation (Buddhism) 2. Buddhism

Printed in Sri Lanka by
Karunaratne & Sons Ltd.
67 U.D.A., Industrial Estate
Homagama

THE WHEEL PUBLICATION NO. 441/442

CONTENTS

Preface

The Way to The Happiness of Peace was published many years ago under a different title, *The Principles of Satipaṭṭhāna Vipassanā*. They were talks given by Sayadaw U Panditabhivamsa while I was in Myanmar. It has now been freshly edited by Bodhisāra and Sumangalo for re-publication.

This collection of talks is a comprehensive teaching of Buddhist practice in brief. The Dhamma is timeless. That which has been said then is still as relevant to us today. What has been learnt has to be learnt by newcomers to the practice. Veterans should have frequent reminders of what has been said before.

May all who come to the Dhamma put it into practice and reap its benefits to the best of their ability.

SUJIVA

Santisukharama
Kota Tinggi, Johor
12 December 1996

CHAPTER ONE

The Culture of the Buddha

The *Buddha's dispensation (buddha-sāsana)* is the instructions given by him for self-development in thought, speech, and bodily actions. It could perhaps be more appropriately rendered as the Buddha's *culture* or *refinement*. To be truly cultured or civilized requires the ability to restrain oneself from all harmful actions directed towards living beings through the three doors of mind, speech, and body.

To be able to restrain the mind requires the ability to differentiate wholesome from unwholesome actions. This is the cultivation of wisdom. If an action is harmful yet one still does it, then one is uncivilized. If an action is harmful but one restrains oneself from doing it, then one is civilized.

One should place oneself in another person's shoes when contemplating any harmful actions. The Buddha instructed that one has to put oneself in the position of a mother of other beings to understand them. Expressed poetically, we could then say the teaching lies in the heart.

Keeping the Five Precepts is the way to be cultured in all physical acts. It is called ***the culture of moral integrity***. Other religions too have such guidelines to moral purification.

There is a controversy about the last precept, the abstinence from alcohol, when it comes to small quantities, especially during social drinking. But even small amounts are often risky temptations. Where should we draw the line between a little bit and too much? Transgressing this rule is a frequent cause for the breaking of the other four precepts.

Considering the faults and pains in disregarding the precepts helps us to shun breaking them. Considering the benefits of keeping precepts encourages us to observe them. Perfection in moral integrity indicates a high level of true civilization. Yet, although one's precepts are kept pure, unwholesome states of mind can still arise. That is, *the mind* is still uncivilized and barbaric. To be mentally civilized, we have to go to the next step—***the culture of concentration.***

The culture of concentration falls into two categories, tranquillity meditation (*samatha bhāvanā*) and insight meditation (*vipassanā bhāvanā*). This exposition will be mainly concerned with the culture of insight meditation. When one notes mindfully the bodily processes, the mind ceases to wander. At that moment, there are no thoughts of aggression, lust, or breaking the precepts. The mind is clear and pure. The three factors—energy, mindfulness, and concentration—contribute to a truly cultured mind. This is moral integrity which comes about through concentration. To really enjoy the benefits of such a cultured mind, one should fully resolve to be serious and continuous in one's practice.

The main benefit of insight meditation is the seeing of things according to their true nature—seeing that all that exists are conditioned mental and material phenomena and that these are impermanent, oppressive, and governed by impersonal laws. This insight culminates in the attainment of the first stage of enlightenment, which has the important function of eliminating forever certain classes of unwholesome consciousness. This culmination marks the establishment of ***the culture of understanding,*** which is the Buddha's teaching not outside of us but in our hearts.

Two factors contribute greatly to such a noble aim, the faithful listening to instructions given by the teacher and the serious application of the teaching in one's practice.

CHAPTER TWO

The Way to the Happiness of Peace

The way to the *happiness of peace*[1] has three strands in the basic, the preliminary, and the Noble Path.

The Basic Path

To enter the ***basic path*** one must gain a proper understanding of the fundamental right view on kamma, which holds that moral actions always beget wholesome results and immoral actions always beget unwholesome results. It is on the basis of this understanding that one follows the morality which is in accordance with the Eightfold Path. One leads a virtuous life, cultivating good intentions, effort, speech, and livelihood, and is mindful of the higher things in life. By "good" we mean that which is conducive to the extinction of defilements.

This right view on kamma, however, can not only become absent in individuals but may get lost even in whole societies. Still, it will not disappear altogether from the surface of the world. If it vanishes in one country, it will to some degree spring up in another. For this reason, it is also called *the light of the world*, or the *light of saṁsāra*, the round of birth and death. The benefit derived from this right view is the ability to avoid evil deeds and to perform good actions with strong determination.

---

1. In Pali: *santisukha*. *Santi:* peace, *sukha:* happiness. This is the happiness of the peace of Nibbāna, contrary to the limited happiness gained from sensual pleasures or meditative states.

The Preliminary Path and the Noble Path

In meditation centres yogis, bent on avoiding evil and doing good, usually observe eight precepts. Such a wholesome and moral life is essential to the serious practice of mindfulness and concentration. The dedicated observance of precepts frees one from the gross faults of greed, hatred, and delusion. There arises momentary peace from the defilements. This also occurs when one is noting phenomena arising at the six sense doors. For example, while watching the rising and falling of the abdomen, the transgressive defilements as well as those that occur at the mental level do not arise. With continued exertion of energy the power of observation will gather momentum. The defilements are more easily kept away.

What matters most is that the drive against the defilements is constant and vigilant. Otherwise one may drift in the opposite direction, towards laziness, unmindfulness, and distractedness.

The application of energy may be described with the use of a simile: It is like filling an empty, narrow-necked bottle (full of air) with water. Each drop removes a little air. But because the mouth is small, one needs to be accurate and careful to ensure that the drops fall straight in.

Like the vacuum flask which can keep the water cool for a long time, one should likewise be able to keep the mind free from defilements for a long time. When there is the right object at the right time and one is able to go on noting, one will begin to gain insight[2] into mind and matter, their causal relationship and so on, until one reaches the ***Noble Path*** where the relevant defilements are completely uprooted.

---

2. In Pali: *vipassanā.* It is the deep, intuitive seeing or understanding of impermanence, suffering, and non-self in all conditioned things. Reflective or superficial insight *(We are all growing old ...)* does not amount to vipassanā insight.

The practice of mindfulness in the ***preliminary path*** is none other than the mind-training given by the Buddha in the *Discourse on the Four Foundations of Mindfulness*[3] (see pp.8ff.). If one practises the foundations of mindfulness seriously, then one treads the Noble Eightfold Path itself:

a. The careful noting at the sense doors, for example the occurrences of the rising and falling at the belly, has to be done with effort. This is *Right Effort.*

b. One ensures that nothing escapes mindfulness, for example one closely notes every sound, every painful sensation, etc. This is *Right Mindfulness.*

c. While noting the object mindfully, the mind concentrates intently on the noted object. This is *Right Concentration.*

These three factors constitute the ***concentration group*** of the Eightfold Path.

d. While watching the rising of the abdomen the mind is aware of the characteristics of the primary elements—such as hardness, heat, and motion. It is also aware of the arising and vanishing of these characteristics, of their unsatisfactory nature, and the absence of anyone controlling their occurrence. This knowledge arises in meditators not because the meditation teacher speaks about it and not through study, but intuitively, based on direct personal experience. This is *Right View.*

e. At the time of observation the mind must attend to the right object in the right way. This is *Right Aim,* which is free from wrong aim at thoughts of sensual desire, ill-will, and cruelty.

These two factors make up the ***wisdom group*** of the Path.

---

3. Satipaṭṭhāna Sutta, Majjhima Nikāya No. 10

f. During his retreat a meditator abstains from lying, slanderous speech, harsh speech, and idle chatter. This fulfils *Right Speech.*

g. On retreat one also abstains from taking life, stealing, sexual misconduct, taking intoxicants, etc. This is *Right Action.*

h. In abstaining from wrong speech and wrong action in earning one's living, one also satisfies the conditions for *Right Livelihood.*

These last three factors constitute the ***moraliy group*** of the Path.

A meditator also develops during insight meditation the understanding of the *Four Noble Truths.*

This is illustrated as follows:

i. While trying to observe the rising and falling of the abdomen, pain, restlessness, etc., are noticed. These things are suffering. One comes to know what there is to be known about the ***truth of suffering*** inherent in all conditioned things.

ii. In meditation one is abandoning the ***cause of suffering,*** namely, craving with its companions ignorance and anger.

iii. There comes about a momentary extinction of defilements, which is the mundane ***truth of the cessation of suffering.***

iv. And of course the ***truth of the path*** is being developed with each moment of proper mindfulness.

CHAPTER THREE

Basic Principles of Insight Practice

Before commencing insight meditation (*vipassanā bhāvanā*), it is advisable to practise the *four guardian meditations.*

Recollection of the Buddha

One recollects the special virtues of the Buddha. One can select just one of the many qualities and reflect on it. For example, the Buddha has the quality of an *arahant*, a perfected one. A brief contemplation is sufficient.

At some phases of one's meditation one may meet with fearsome objects. This recollection helps to overcome such fear.

Cultivation of Loving Kindness

In this practice one develops friendliness towards all beings using the concise phrase:

May all beings be free from enmity.

One radiates loving kindness to all beings repeatedly. The short and concise phrase has a wide range in meaning. For example, *enmity* refers both to internal enemies (i.e., defilements) and external enemies (unfriendly beings, dangers, etc.). If people are really free from enmity, then there is true peace in humanity. Such a practice creates a friendly atmosphere around oneself and therefore one will not be harassed or disturbed by other beings.

Recollection of Loathsomeness

In the recollection of loathsomeness one need not refer to corpses. One can refer to the loathsomeness of the living body. Normally people have a lot of attachment to *bodies*, their own or others. If one really looks closely into the body's parts, one can loosen the attachment to it.

For example, reflect on head hair, body hair, nails, teeth, skin.

The perception of loathsome with regard to the body helps to overcome lust, which may arise as a strong hindrance in the meditation practice.

Recollection of Death

Frequent recollection of the inevitable nature of death irrespective of caste, rank, age, place, etc., cultivates a sense of fearlessness of death together with an increased sense of urgency to purify the mind and practise the foundations of mindfulness. One will also be able to endure excruciating sensations that arise in the course of one's practice.

For those who intend to practise insight meditation, these four guardian meditations may occupy a total of eight minutes (i.e., two minutes each) once or several times a day at the beginning of a round of sitting meditation.

In insight meditation mindfulness establishes itself with firmness and continuous occurrence in four domains of mind and body. This establishment is called ***four foundations of mindfulness***.

Contemplation of the Body

This is the repeated observation of the material qualities in the body. Four postures are used when one contemplates the body. For the beginner the sitting and walking postures are suitable because the standing posture needs a lot of energy and can be too demanding for the beginner, and the lying posture easily leads one to fall asleep. Sitting and walking, on the other hand, are most suitable for the balancing of faculties. In the sitting posture the body is allowing concentration to develop, yet a certain amount of energy is required to keep it upright. Walking increases the faculty of energy and helps to balance out the strong tranquillity developed in sitting still.

Traditionally, sitting is done cross-legged. If done awkwardly, a lot of pain may arise within a short time, so it should be done carefully and properly. The trunk should be erect, preferably perpendicular. This prevents the arising of unnecessary painful feelings. It also helps blood circulation.

> Seated cross-legged,
> with straight back;
> the mind centered
> on the belly.

After sitting like this, place the mindfulness on the basic meditation object, *the rising and falling process of the abdomen.* Watching the rise and fall enables one to find the natural phenomena which can be seen in their true nature.

To bring forth penetration or insight into the phenomena one has to be in the right place at the right time. The right place is the process of *rising* or *falling* of the abdomen. The right time is their *very moment of occurrence.*

The mind is too readily swept away by defilements. By fixing the mind on the rising and falling of the abdomen, the mind is temporarily freed from them. This, of course, initially requires a lot of effort.

A simile: A little boat is easily swept downstream but to get it upstream is difficult. To make it go upstream one must first manipulate the rudder, which compares with the placing of the mindfulness on the belly. After that one needs to row, that means one needs to follow the rising and falling uninterruptedly and relentlessly with continuous effort, to move upstream.

For this, two kinds of power are required: *Energetic power,* which is the complete and relentless effort to follow the rising and falling, and *accurate power,* which is the accuracy in the following. Accuracy comes from hitting each and every occurring phenomenon with right mindfulness. The breathing rhythm should be normal and natural and not forced. When these two powers of effort and accuracy are balanced, there is momentary concentration.

The procedure may be compared to a spider in its web. Normally the spider is poised at the centre of the web. Whenever an insect gets caught, it rushes to it, saps its nutrition, and returns to the centre. Likewise the meditator puts the attention on the centre, the primary object of observation, the rising and falling of the abdomen. Whenever any other object arises the mind takes quick note of it, due to the power of effort and accuracy.

> Breathing
> naturally,
> fix the mind on
> rising and falling.

In each moment of careful attention and precise noting of the rising and failing of the abdomen the mental factors for the elimination of defilements are developed.

These factors are:

i. Right Effort, which has the function of not accepting defilements.
ii. Right Aim, which has the function of applying the mind accurately on the desired object, putting it right on the target.
iii. Right Mindfulness, which has the function of guarding the mind from defilements.
iv. Right Concentration, which has the function of preventing the mind from being scattered.

The mind thus is in a pure state. This itself is virtue and goodness, benefits that arise simultaneously with every moment of mindfulness. Therefore at every noting in meditation one is cultivating the skilful and wholesome mind.

Pure dwells
the mind,
free from guilt,
and in true virtue.

When we begin our practice, we start to see how wild the mind is—like a kid neglected by his parents. If we leave the mind in this state, we will not be free of obstacles blocking our spiritual growth, as we are under constant bombardment by objects giving rise to pleasant and unpleasant feelings, thus to greed, hatred, and delusion. This reactive mind can only be tamed by proper mind control.

If parents, for example, do not exercise control over their children, they may, through the influence of bad company, become juvenile delinquents. However, if proper control is exercised, the children would eventually mature in wisdom and gain the discretion to keep away from unskilful actions, even at times when their parents are not around.

It is the same with meditation. The mind now and again runs after sensual desires, gets upset. We need to control it and allow it to grow up. This period of discipline, though painful, is necessary.

Despite initial resentment in the child's mind, it will eventually come to realize the benefits of wise control as a basis for a successful life. Becoming independent, the control will then come from within, no longer having to be imposed from outside, and the child will know how to discern wholesome from unwholesome actions and keep to the good throughout life.

At the beginning, it is difficult to centre the mind on the rising and falling of the abdomen. But it is reassuring to know that the invested effort and discipline provide space to grow and develop skilfulness. This difficult technique of attentive mind control is essential for mental purity. This is what meditation means: the cultivation of skilful states which enable wisdom to blossom.

What do we mean by insight and wisdom? When the hindrances to concentration are absent for longer periods of time, one can see natural phenomena directly, for example the movement, stiffness, heat, sensations, etc. in the rising and falling of the abdomen. As one goes further, one begins to be able to differentiate between mental and physical phenomena occurring within the field of awareness. Furthermore, the intricate chain of conditioning of phenomena can also be discerned.

Stiffness, tension,
movement,
and displacement:
discern them all.

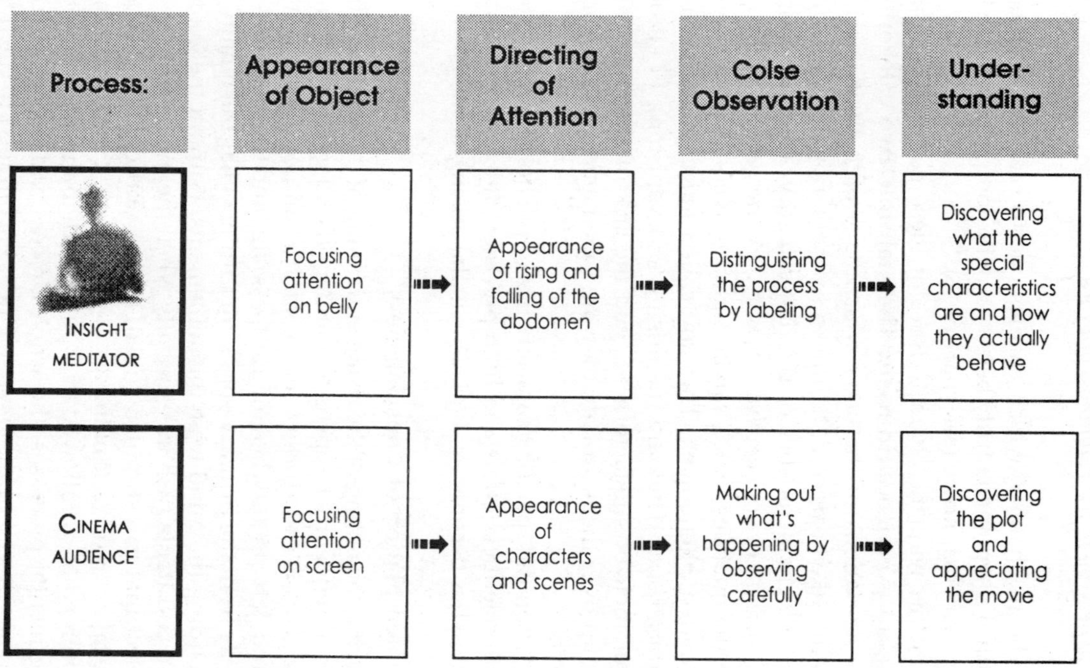
Process:
Appearance of Object
Directing of Attention
Colse Observation
Under-standing
Insight Meditator
Focusing attention on belly
Appearance of rising and falling of the abdomen
Distinguishing the process by labeling
Discovering what the special characteristics are and how they actually behave
Cinema Audience
Focusing attention on screen
Appearance of characters and scenes
Making out what's happening by observing carefully
Discovering the plot and appreciating the movie

The mechanism which enables one to see how all these natural phenomena truly behave can be compared to watching a cinema movie (see chart p. 13).

In this way, the characteristics of these natural phenomena are experienced directly. They fall into two categories. The sensations of the body which have each their specific quality like heat, cold, hardness, softness, flowing, pressure, etc., are characteristics of the first category. They are called the *specific* or *unique characteristics.* In the second category are the qualities which can be found universally in all compounded phenomena. They are called *universal* or *common characteristics.* They are the arising and vanishing of all objects, their unsatisfactoriness, and the lack of absolute ownership over them. In Pali, they are called *anicca, dukkha,* and *anattā.*

When the specific characteristics of phenomena are noted with relentless effort and high precision, the universal characteristics become evident. This is the arising of insight.

Contemplation of Consciousness

During the noting of the rising and falling of the abdomen the mind frequently happens to wander off and get lost in thinking. This is called *wandering mind.* It is an occurrence of the mind. It happens when mindfulness slips and the mind moves away from the primary object. Mindfulness has the quality of guarding the mind from the defilements. Without the guardian, pollutants rush in, especially when the mind turns to an object that can stimulate greed, hatred, and delusion. When we take careful note of the wandering mind, it disappears and is immediately followed by a pure mind. In the course of noting mental processes, the whole process and nature of consciousness can be discovered. One is encouraged to catch the very moment the mind starts wandering.

Wandering thoughts,
miss them not,
note them all,
on the spot.

Can one gain any benefit from watching negative mind states like anger or greed? Would they not turn on us and gain power over us? The teachings tell us that by being with the present moment, not only can one see their true nature, one can also put a stop to the defilements. This is just as, by being watchful of infiltrators or guerrillas, the police can stop their activities.

The untrained mind is naturally wild and easily possessed by negative mental states. It is not useful, like an untamed horse for the owner. The wild mind can be characterized in three ways: it is difficult to tame; it is extremely quick and merely skims superficially over what is really happening; and it is capricious and frivolous. Therefore it is treacherous and painful to the owner. For these reasons the Buddha praises the taming of the unruly, wild mind. How to tame it? One tames it as one does a wild elephant. First, one has to catch hold of it in the place where it originates from, the wild jungle. Similarly, one catches the mind where it originates, at the six sense doors. One has to be with each moment of occurrence at whatever door it arises—the eye, ear, nose, tongue, body, or mind door—persistently and relentlessly. Only then can one experience peace never experienced before.

In the Pali texts it is said: *Bhūtaṁ bhūtato passati.* This can be translated as: One looks at things as they really are/occur. *Things* refer to all the conditioned phenomena and must be things that can be directly experienced, for example, the mental intention to sit down and the whole physical process of sitting down that follows.

In the beginning one uses the help of labelling the object as it really occurs. For example, one mentally labels as *intending* (to sit) when there is intention and then *sitting* when the process of sitting occurs. Or *rising* for the rising process of the abdomen, and *falling* for the falling process of the abdomen. When one is directing attention to the rising and falling of the abdomen which is caused by gross breathing, one is able to distinguish the form or shape of the belly, the modes of disposition, and the sensations that are felt through bare experience. *Rising* and *falling* are modes of disposition. When noting these modes of disposition, with the improvement of practice, one experiences them as *bare sensations* such as tension, hardness, motion, heat, pain, etc.

During the Buddha's time the concise instruction of *bhūtaṁ bhūtato passati* was sufficient for people with keen wisdom, who could act on simple and bare guidance to gain insight. Later this type of people became rare and therefore teachers of the commentaries explained the necessity of labelling as a supportive tool in steadying the awareness and clarifying the nature of the observed object.

There is an argument which says that labelling is actually an introduction of a new set of concepts and contradicts the actual instruction of seeing things as they really are. The commentaries refer to a certain type of concept, *appropriate concept.* For example, heat can be felt without naming or labelling, but there is a name concept for it: *heat* in English, or *uṇha* in Pali. This concept can be used by beginners in insight meditation, whose concentration and mindfulness are not yet developed strongly, as a tool to direct the mind to the object. With the deepening of practice, the labels are automatically dropped and the mind will experience its object free from concepts. The labelling helps to keep the noting mind in order—as a ruler held below a line of writing on the page helps a child learning to read.

When insight matures, especially at the strong fourth and fifth insight knowledges, there is a sudden increase in the rate of what is happening. It is so fast that one does not have time to label. Then there will be only bare awareness of phenomena, sensations without shape, form, or mode of disposition.

At this point, the yogi has two choices: either one continues labelling, or one just allows the mind to flow with what is happening without using labels. When the student wants to keep labelling, only part of the quickly arising and disappearing phenomena can be labelled, not all. The second method is preferable, because if one continues trying to label, there is a tendency for fatigue to set in quite soon.

Only if one can catch the phenomena on the spot does one see *things as they really are*. "Only" is important because it emphasizes the present moment. There is no place for thinking, reflection, speculation, or interpretation. One has to be with the moment, with the here and now on the spot, not before or after. Just as, if one is to behold a bolt of lightning, one has to watch it at the moment it occurs. Lean your weight on one side (with a hand resting on the floor and the arm propping up the body) and label *supporting*. Close your eyes and at the same time put your whole attention onto the mode of the body posture.

After some time, you can experience stiffness, tension, discomfort, vibrations, heat, hardness, or similar sensations. The labelling is simply a skilful tool to direct and fix the attention on a chosen object so that the real characteristics can become evident.

Contemplation of Feelings

Good, bad, and
neutral feelings.
Bungle not!
Note! Note!

Painful Feelings

While the yogi is engaged in his work of mindfulness discomfort is frequently encountered, such as itches, aches, pain, and the like.

To overcome discomfort, one has to be at the very moment of its occurrence so that one can see into its true nature. For if one does not note, one cannot be aware of it and might be deluded to think that "I am in pain." Furthermore, the mind usually reacts to pain with anger or disappointment, so one suffers unnecessarily. This is what happens when one *thinks about* the pain and *reacts* to it rather than just *stays with* it. One should not multiply the suffering, but should firmly and composedly watch and penetrate it.

Every time one is not mindful of a painful sensation as it occurs, anger arises, followed by unhappiness and oppression. In addition, one is also likely to crave for pleasant sensation. This is disguised as hope.

For example, when one drinks dirty water, one suffers not only by having to drink it but also from wishing for clean water. This wish is another form of suffering. When the diligent effort to look into these sensations is insufficient, a lot of aversion and hopeful feelings will arise. So one should be firmly resolved and endeavour to look at the pain. Then its true nature will emerge.

Energy is a wonderful quality that can arouse the mindfulness to have a good look at the pain. It can also bring about collectedness of mind and penetration into the object. When this happens, then there is no chance for anger and wishful thinking to arise. With the deepening of practice one can even lose the perception of the body form. Then there is just the noting mind and the various bare sensations. At that time the mindfulness is exact and impeccable. And one can have good meditation despite all the pain. This is an evidence of *equipoise,* the supreme quality of meditative penetration. This wonderful quality is developed when there is relentless effort, collectedness of mind, and accuracy of application on the desired object at every moment.

But before insight matures, the observed pain may increase to such an extent that one comes to think one has never experienced so much pain before. As a result, doubt about the practice and regret about having started it might arise. What really happens is that the pain is magnified by the power of concentration. Watching insects with a magnifying glass makes them also look huge and dangerous.

At this stage it is essential to be patient and cultivate a heroic effort to watch the pain being experienced. With the deepening of insight there will very likely be non-identification with the pain. Then there will be only bare noting and bare sensations. One must not be afraid of pain or even death. In all of Sayadaw's experience there has not been a single person who died because of his encounter with pain in the course of meditation. One should therefore be like a fearless warrior.

The other quality to cultivate here is patience. This practice is indeed a good test of valour, patience, and strength of mind. So try your very best not to move and give in. Just freeze and watch. Once one is able to overcome this initial difficulty, then one has gained confidence in one's own strength and effort. A lot of energy and concentration will also build up. This victory over fear and oppression by pain develops good qualities. One will have real appreciation for the work of insight and is very likely to encounter special experiences in the future.

Pleasant Feelings

Pleasant feelings arise in both body and mind as comfort and happiness. If one is not mindful when they arise, one tends to be swayed by craving. One wishes them to last longer and this gives rise to never-ending desire. The Buddha taught that feelings are a condition for craving. One therefore should check this link by noting it at the very moment of its occurrence. When doing so, one can also penetrate into its true nature.

There are two types of pleasant sensations, *worldly pleasant sensations,* such as those induced by good sights, sounds, odours, tastes, touches, and thoughts, and *pleasant sensations* that are strictly *concerned with meditation.* The latter ones arise when the practice deepens. One experiences tremendous peace and calm. There is also a lot of buoyancy and satisfaction. The mind becomes bright and alert. These pleasant experiences are quite remote from sensual pleasures, but if the yogi is still not well-trained, there remains a tendency to get attached to them.

The Buddha once posed a riddle for one who is bent on peace:

> One neither allows the mind to wander outside nor to stop inside. If one is able to do that one will experience true peace.

Wandering outside means to be careless when sensual objects strike the eye, ear, nose, etc., and the mind runs after them. It is like a child up to mischief behind the parents' back. If the parents are wise and understanding, they can help by being strict. Therefore, one must try to free the mind through disciplined attention from mindless running after sense pleasures.

Actually, the pleasant sensation arising at the moment an external object contacts the mind is kammically indeterminate. The danger lies in the *reaction* to it, for example, when one allows craving for a continued experience of it to arise. So the first step is to be mindful and clean up any possible reaction. As a result the mind becomes bright and peaceful. Many pleasant sensations such as thrills and rapture will follow. One may even enter stages of extreme calmness and coolness. Again there is a danger of a lot of satisfaction arising after allowing a subtle form of craving to creep in. This is called *stopping inside* or *stagnating within.* The antidote is again to be mindful and note every arising.

If a traveller is on a journey to meet a friend, she cannot afford to stop too long at some pleasant places along the way. Doing so, she may be exposing herself to dangers and miss the appointment. So she has to go according to the schedule.

After the yogi has overcome this subtle craving, he needs to keep on noting whatever arises. Impeccable mindfulness which prevents wandering outside and stagnating inside will lead to the true happiness for which one aspires.

Neutral Feelings

It is natural for pleasant feelings to arise after meeting with an agreeable object and unpleasant feelings after meeting with a disagreeable object. Similarly, neutral feelings follow after meeting with a neither agreeable nor disagreeable object. However, it is difficult for beginners to spot these indifferent or neutral feelings. Daily one meets with a lot of neutral objects. For example, one may glance at a stone or a pebble. At the very moment of contact there is neutral feeling. It also occurs with sounds, smells, tastes, touch sensations, and thoughts. In the instructions for the beginner, one is told to concentrate on prominent objects. Among the feelings one should watch are pleasant feelings and painful feelings rather than neutral feelings.

As practice deepens, one will be able to distinguish these more subtle indifferent feelings too. They become very distinct starting from the insight knowledge of dissolution up to the insight knowledge of equanimity about formations, where they become most obvious. This latter stage is a peaceful and tranquil state where one has a lot of energy and can silently watch and meditate for long hours. At this point again one can easily become attached to the tranquillity and may convince oneself that one has at last attained to the Special Dhamma.

But as long as one is still clinging to good practice there is a tendency to stagnate. The strategy to combat subtle attachment is to be very mindful of the specific and universal characteristics of neutral feelings. For the yogi at the stage of equanimity about formations it is even more important to be continuous and relentless in the effort throughout the day. Having overcome this attachment, one may experience a jump into emptiness while clearly watching the object; that means a disappearing of the noting mind.

Contemplation of Mental Objects

Mental objects here can be interpreted as *natural phenomena* which are experienced directly through any of the six sense doors and are empty of a permanent entity.

The Process of Seeing

Firstly, let us investigate a set of prominent mental objects involved in the act of seeing. The process may be compared to the striking of a match (striker) on the box (receptor) to produce a flame (ignition). There are three component parts present for it to occur:

a. the visual object (striker)

b. the eye basis (receptor)

c. the seeing consciousness (ignition)

The receptor or the sensitivity of the eye is a natural phenomenon. It is the sensitive material basis for the reception of the visual object. It is egoless and liable to change. At the moment of contact between the striker (visual object) and receptor (eye basis), there is ignition (the seeing consciousness). The striker and the ignition, like the receptor, are egoless and liable to change. Each of these phenomena also has its peculiar or unique characteristics. These three elements occur *simultaneously* during the act of seeing.

In meditation this act can be noted in a general way with the use of the convenient label *seeing*. When noting it, the mind will be able to pick up any one of the three elements which happens to be predominant at that particular moment. If one is able to take note in this way, one is said to be contemplating mental objects. One has to penetrate the unique characteristics and see the cause and effect relationship between these elements. If one is not mindful and does not see the impersonality of these natural phenomena, one is overcome by ignorance. Heedlessness is also the cause of craving for any of the three elements to arise. One may crave to see, be attached to the eye, or feel lust for the object seen. When craving increases it turns into grasping, to indulgence in sensuality, and the wrong belief in a self or soul.

Fear arises because clinging knows no bounds. Clinging is a *sticky attachment*. The knowing frees one from craving. There are two prominent characteristics with these *sticky defilements*. They are *oppressive* mental objects. There arises a lot of frustration while trying to get the objects craved for. There is also a lot of suffering from the possessive guarding of obtained objects and the inevitable separation from them either during one's lifetime or at the moment of death.

The defilements are like *strong heat*. Craving, clinging, lust, etc., burn like a fire. The mind is burning while scheming to get something or even more when one is unsuccessful in getting it. A fire burns off the fuel leaving only filth and ashes. Similarly, defilements burn us, leaving our minds dirty and unhappy. Knowing this, let one build up an efficient and effective defence, mobilizing the fire brigade of mindfulness to put out the raging fire of defilements.

> Not knowing, one clings;
> clinging brings fear.
> Knowing is freeing;
> freedom is clear peace.

The Process of Hearing

At the moment of hearing there also occur three elements:

a. sound (striker)

b. ear base (receptor)

c. hearing consciousness (ignition)

If one is unmindful, there is ignorance and therefore one tends to cling to pleasant sounds or has aversion to sounds one does not like. One tends to think that *I am hearing*, and one gets attached to the physical ear as well. Unless one is mindful, one cannot successfully penetrate into their true nature.

When one is unmindful, three cycles start running, the cycles of *defilements*, of *actions*, and of *results*.

For example, one might hear a sweet singing sound of a person of the opposite sex. If one is not mindful, one first clings to the sound. If unchecked, one clings also to the song. Further, there can be a shift of clinging to the singer and all these types of clinging perpetuate the *cycle of defilements*. This leads to desire for possession, which will result in a lot of scheming and actions which are fuel for the *cycle of actions*. One might even resort to illegal and immoral means to obtain the craved objects. All this is bound to make us reap kammic results. This is the *cycle of results*.

Therefore, if one does not nip the defilements in the bud, the cycles will start rolling and create a lot of becoming: continued rebirths and suffering. But if one is in the habit of being mindful and at once notes the process as hearing, one would at times be able to notice the most prominent one of the three elements. One might penetrate intuitively into the true nature of that element. Then the cycle of defilements will be cut off. So will the cycle of actions and their results. The same principle applies to the conscious processes occurring at the other sense doors.

> Seeing, hearing,
> sensing and knowing.
> Don't be careless.
> Note! Note!

The Process of Touching

When one is watching the rising and falling process of the abdomen the three elements are likewise present. The *body base* is like the receptor, the *sensations* manifested as tension, tightness, movement, vibrations, relaxation and so on are like the striker, and the *body* or *touching consciousness* is like the ignition. The purpose of watching the processes is to penetrate deeply into the nature of these three elements.

The defilements we mentioned above can be classified into three types by way of intensity. The grossest are the ***defilements of transgression***, that is, the breaking of one's precepts, or the stepping over the rights of others. The medium gross defilements are ***obsessive defilements*** that occur purely at the mental level and do not manifest in physical action or speech. The most subtle ***defilements lie latent,*** having the potential to arise given the appropriate conditions.

In taking the five or eight precepts lay people on retreat accomplish the three path factors of right action, speech, and livelihood. This pure conduct has the quality of abandoning the defilements of transgression. The right effort, mindfulness, and concentration which are also developed have the ability to abandon defilements at the mental level. But it requires right aim and right understanding, the two factors of the insight group of the Eightfold Path, in a developed form, to cut off the latent defilements. Therefore, when one practises the foundations of mindfulness, every time one is clearly aware of the observed object, there is purification of the defilements at the three levels. Even if one has still yet to reach the state of nobility through enlightenment, the latent tendencies are temporarily abandoned in the sense that they have no room to arise.

The latent defilements can be understood in two ways. As impurities that can arise within the continuity of existence of a being in saṁsāra; they arise when conditions are favourable for their arising. They are called *latent defilements in continuity*. Or they can be understood as impurities that can arise in connection with all clear objects of mind and body. They arise when the conditions are favourable and when the perceived objects are not understood through vipassana insight as they really are. These are called *latent defilements in objects*. Latent defilements can only be uprooted by the noble attainment of enlightenment.

It is these three types of defilements that cause turmoil and conflicts in those whom they afflict. True missionary work involves first the establishment of the Dhamma in oneself before one can share it with others. Only when one is at peace with oneself will one also be at peace with others. This peace will shine forth from one's own heart and encompass the hearts of others. Without the practice of insight meditation one is like a dry parched desert. Existence is meaningless. But one who is established in mindfulness and insight is like an oasis that is cool, fresh, and alive.

The Process of Knowing

The process at the mind door is similar to that of the eye or ear door (see above) since three different elements give rise to mental processes:

a. the mental object (striker)

b. the mind element (receptor)

c. the mind consciousness element (ignition)

The *mental objects* include five sensitivities (which are eye base, ear base, nose, tongue and body base); sixteen subtle material qualities (including the water element); all classes of consciousness; all mental factors; Nibbāna and concepts. All these are ultimate realities, except for concepts.

Two classes of consciousness make up the *mind element*: life-continuum consciousness (*bhavanga citta)* which occurs during deep dreamless sleep, and the mind-door adverting consciousness.

The *mind consciousness element* includes all classes of consciousness which can imagine or think, like seeing images, visions, hallucinations in the mind, hearing sounds in the mind, and the like.

The *material basis* for the mind is the *heart base.* Although not specifically named, it is stated in the Abhidhamma Pitaka that consciousness and the associated mental factors have a material basis. Commentators say that this material basis is located in the clear blood found within the anatomical heart: thus the term *heart base.* Modern science, however, refers its site to the brain. One may question how the latter assertion is possible since the rebirth consciousness arises simultaneously with this material basis and at that time, just after the moment of fertilization, the brain, eyes, etc., have yet to develop. If one's insight develops, one can experience directly the site of the mind consciousness element within the heart.

All objects arising at the mind door, with the exception of concepts and Nibbāna, can be used for insight practice. That is, one should note all activities of the mind. If one is not mindful while thinking, one tends to think that there is someone behind the process. But if one is mindful, one will know that there is actually no one, no self or soul which is thinking. There are just mental phenomena behaving according to their true nature: impermanent, unsatisfactory, and egoless.

Mental objects occupy a very wide range. Here we shall look at five categories.

i. At the moment of *seeing* it is possible that the yogi when concentrated and mindful picks up the eye sensitivity in one of the three ways, that is, as the sensitivity that allows visual objects in, as the connection between the seeing consciousness and the visual object, or as the physical basis upon which the seeing process depends. The same can be applied to the other sensitivities.

ii. When experiencing physical sensations such as trickling, solidity, heat, hardness, etc., one may experience them in lumps. This *cohesive quality is* actually the characteristic of the *element of water.* It is always experienced together with another element, like hardness (earth element), heat (fire element), or pressure (air element). While watching the cohesion one is contemplating a mental object, as the water element cannot be directly experienced at the body door.

iii. One object for the contemplation of mental objects is picked up usually after meals: the *nutritive essence.* It can be felt as increased strength, together with fullness of the belly and tightness of the body.

iv. One is also contemplating mental objects when observing the *five hindrances*: sensual desire, ill-will, sloth and torpor, restlessness and worry, and doubt. When craving for attractive objects arises one might come to know of it automatically or one might note it deliberately as *sensual desire.* Then one is contemplating a mental object. While noting, one may come to know the cause for the arising of these hindrances, the cause for overcoming them, and the cause of their eradication. This is also contemplation of mental objects.

v. Included in the field of contemplation of mental objects are the *seven factors of enlightenment,* namely:

1. *Mindfulness*

Mindfulness becomes obvious at the stage of the insight knowledge into arising and passing away of phenomena. At that point it is clear that mindfulness and its corresponding object occur in pairs. This mindfulness is the *enlightenment factor of* ***mindfulness***.

2. *Investigation of States*

Investigation of states actually refers to insight knowledge itself. At times, as intuitive insight knowledge arises, there is a looking back on it and acknowledging it. This is a contemplation of mental objects, that is, watching the *enlightenment factor of* ***investigations of states***.

3. *Energy*

At a certain point in the practice one may notice that even without any deliberate or special exertion effort comes about automatically and evenly. One is then aware of the *enlightenment factor of* ***energy***, which is another instance of contemplation of mental objects.

4. *Joyful Interest*

Similarly when insight knowledge arises, it may occur with various forms of joyful interest or deep satisfaction. When one takes note of this, one is watching the *enlightenment factor of* ***joy***.

5. *Calmness*

Again, at that stage, one also experiences ease of body and mind. Being free from worries one is tranquil. This is the *enlightenment factor of* ***calmness***.

6. *Concentration*

Furthermore, the mind keeps on sinking, penetrating into whatever arises. That is, the mind is not scattered but collected, falling accurately onto the object observed. This is the *enlightenment factor of* ***one-pointed concentration.***

7. *Equanimity*

Lastly, the mind becomes very balanced. It is observantly noting with composure all pleasant and unpleasant phenomena appearing in its field of awareness, without reacting either positively or negatively to them. This balanced state is the *enlightenment factor of* ***equanimity.***

Physiological Benefits

The immediate benefit of the practice of the foundations of mindfulness is the development of the seven factors of enlightenment, which eventually will lead to the utter release from suffering. A by-product of the practice are changes in material phenomena. In the Saṃyutta Nikāya the Buddha once commented that one who has regrets and remorse over the past, and worries and craving for the future, will not be blessed with health, beauty, and the like. But if one does not have remorse, worry, or craving for things of the past and future, but is easily satisfied, then one will have a complexion that is pleasant and clear.

When a yogi is engrossed in insight meditation, he is, with every moment of mindfulness, developing special qualities manifested as light, joyful contentment, and other non-sensual ecstasies. One becomes very calm, and with the deepening of practice, mindfulness and insight arise to abandon the mental defilements. This also brings about a radical change for the better in the physiological system, especially in the blood circulation. As a result there is heightened awareness and sensitivity through the sense organs. What is more, there have also been cases of yogis being cured of many chronic ailments and diseases. I will cite two cases.

Case A

Fifteen years ago at the Mahasi branch centre in Moulmein, Myanmar, there was a man suffering from stomach ulcer. He had been advised by a physician to undergo a surgical operation. Being afraid that he might die, he decided to put it off and went to do meditation instead. After one week, he had a relapse and he suffered intense pain. If not for the teacher's encouragement, he would have given up.

By the third week he felt the ulcer stiffen, which gave rise to a lot of pain. But by then the concentration and mindfulness had increased and he could endure it. At one point he lost all sense of bodily form and there was only the mindful consciousness noting pain. There was detachment while watching phenomena arising and passing away.

Then once he heard a loud sound of the ulcer bursting. He was cured of the ailment! He no longer had to avoid certain types of food, nor to undergo the operation. After the retreat his eyes and skin became very clear and bright. He had even put on weight. Ever since he has been helping the Buddha's dispensation in many ways.

Case B

There was a lady who had high blood pressure for thirty years. She had spent a lot of money consulting physicians but to no avail. About ten years ago she came to practise meditation in the meditation centre.

After a while there was a lot of tension and pain in her brain, and at times she felt as if the blood vessels were at the point of bursting. Though her relatives pleaded with her to go back, she endured the pain and continued the practice of pinpointing the pain whenever it arose, until she even felt giddy at times. Later a lot of heat began to emanate, together with profuse sweating, followed by a stinking odour coming out of her armpits. As she persisted noting observantly, the heat subsided and her whole body eventually cooled down. After that she was completely cured of high blood pressure.

Many yogis have been cured through the practice of the foundations of mindfulness, that is to say, through the development of the enlightenment factors, especially of ailments connected with the blood, stomach, and nerves. In the Pali Canon, we also come across the Buddha and his close disciples being cured by this practice. Mahakassapa once became ill because of unhealthy food. His sense organs dulled. When the Buddha recited to him the factors of enlightenment he listened and reflected on how he had first become a monk and within one week of practice had penetrated the Four Noble Truths and perfected the development of the seven factors. As a result of this reflection there was an upsurge of joy and he was filled with praise for the Buddha and his teachings. After that his faculties and complexion became very clear.

The factors of enlightenment have great power and potency. They are said to be the most effective medicine. Though this practice of the four foundations of mindfulness is essentially the process of purification of the mind, it can also result in the purification of the body.

CHAPTER FOUR

Arousing Skillful States

We are always surrounded by objects with the potential to elicit unwholesome reactions of the mind. Paying attention to *four avenues of mental habits* can ensure a higher degree of safety in the face of tempting objects. They are essential in arousing skilful states to counteract mental pollutions.

The first habit is ***restriction***. It is the skilful confinement of the mind to wholesome states by means of the strong resolve: "May my mind dwell only in the field of wholesome states."

This is a powerful force which carries on even when one meets with strong objects that tend to stimulate unwholesome mental activities. For example, before one goes to a busy town, one can resolve not to cause an accident. As a result, one drives into town very mindfully. Similarly, one may resolve to abstain from harmful food even though it tastes very nice. In the same way a resolve can restrict the mind to dwell only in the realm of mindfulness.

The second is the habit of ***reorientation***. Despite the resolution of restriction, the mind may still wander to unwholesome states of mind. When this happens, one should quickly disengage from those unwholesome states and reorient it to wholesomeness. That is, one should bring the mind back to the principal object of meditation. For example, a foolish driver may cause one to swerve from one's lane, but afterwards one brings the car back to where it should go. In the practice of insight meditation, one is supposed to note whatever arises, but there are times when one is unable to handle a predominant object effectively. That is to say, the strong object tends to take the mind away to unwholesome states. At such a time, it is wiser to disengage it from the intervening object and reorient it to the primary meditation object. This is really a technique of tranquillity meditation rather than insight meditation. The latter can handle any dominant object for its contemplation.

The third accomplishment of mental habit is called ***consecutive occurrence***. This is a mastery that comes from continuous practice. As a result of uninterrupted mindfulness, one becomes progressively more skilful in maintaining wholesome mental states. There will come a time when one will not be drawn even to a very attractive object. The foundation for this is twofold, in that one has firm confidence in the practice of insight and one's motivation is pure and noble. After the establishment of the foundation one has to exert a lot of effort to develop the power of accuracy and mindfulness. Unbroken mindfulness leads to wholesome states occurring consecutively, culminating in the power of mind to stay unaffected even at times of crisis, and in the realization of impermanence, unsatisfactoriness, and non-self.

The fourth accomplishment is the ability to ***give apt attention*** whenever encountering attractive, repulsive, or delusive objects, as a natural inclination arising from supportive kammic and social conditioning. To be able to develop apt attention four conditions need to be fulfilled. These conditions carry the name of *four wheels of fulfilment*.

i. A *suitable locality* is required, where one can find conducive social conditions that can bring about wholesome actions. That is, one can find the four classes of the Buddha's following—monks, nuns, male and female devotees—and can practise generosity, morality, and meditation. In other words, it is a place where Buddha Dhamma is flourishing and expressed in the life of the people.

ii. Once one has found a suitable locality, then one also needs *suitable company.* The most important people to influence one's spiritual growth are one's parents, teachers, and intimate friends. If one associates with those who are always thinking of others' welfare and are pure in their deeds, not malicious, who hold dhammic values in high esteem, then one is able to develop a lot of spiritual enthusiasm and a sense of urgency to perform meritorious actions. One can also hear a lot of Dhamma and have an opportunity to discuss it regularly.

iii. When, with the help of one's good friends, one has gained understanding of the teachings, then it is up to oneself to value, cherish, and practise these spiritual principles correctly. By *skillful moulding of oneself* one achieves perfection in morality, purity of mind, and insight by penetrating the Dhamma and getting a glimpse of Nibbāna. Then it doesn't matter where one is, because the spiritual values have become an integral part of oneself and will never be lost.

iv. That one has this wonderful opportunity to come across a suitable locality, rely upon good people, and find success in skilfully moulding oneself is because of *one's past meritorious actions.* The results of these past deeds help to create in the present an environment most conducive to spiritual growth.

CHAPTER FIVE

The Ten Armies of Māra

At one time the Buddha addressed his monks: "Listen, monks, I will tell you the weapon that will completely pulverize the army of Māra. It is nothing other than the seven factors of enlightenment."

Meditation is actually a battle between the inner forces of good and evil. Most people are at the mercy of the evil forces.

A weak mind, on meeting with an object likely to trigger off greed, hatred, and delusion, gets swept away by unwholesome tendencies. Therefore, these people are trapped in the vicious cycle of saṁsāra for a long time. One may doubt the possibilities of overcoming evil, but effort is a very potent force. One can use it to conquer the seemingly powerful forces of Māra.[4] Defensive tactics too are needed, and with each step of progress in insight a battle is won. The armed forces of Māra are ten in number.

Māras first army is ***sensual pleasures.*** They fall into the two groups of the sensual objects and the hankering for them. The hankering after these objects is a vicious cycle, a perpetual drowning. One has to overcome it to start treading the path, but total conquest occurs only at the third stage of enlightenment. Although one might not yet have overcome it completely, there is a radical change in one's attitude to-

4. The Pali term *Māra* is derived from a Pali word meaning "death." Māra is the personification of the force of ignorance, delusion, and craving that kills virtue as well as life.

wards these pleasures at the stage of knowledge of rise and fall. Delight in the mental object will make sensual pleasures look cheap.

His second army is ***dissatisfaction.*** Those of you from an affluent society may find the routine in the intensive meditation retreat rather boring. You may also become unhappy with the lower quality of food and the lack of comfort in the meditation centre. But if the dissatisfaction is mindfully noted, one can get over it and carry on with the meditation, the path of purification.

His third is ***hunger and thirst.*** The dissatisfaction will drive the yogi to thirst for good things such as special kinds of facilities or food. But at the stage of insight into rise and fall of phenomena one realizes that the mental object is itself very sumptuous food.

The fourth army is ***craving.*** Craving comes from being deprived of what one likes. Frequent disappointment, for instance in shattered hopes of getting fruits and cakes at lunch or of having something other than rice gruel and beans for breakfast, leads to a frantic effort to search and get what one craves for. But again, at the stage of rise and fall the yogis realize that there is no taste that can beat the taste of the Dhamma. Then there is no more of that familiar hankering.

Sloth and torpor is the fifth army. When one is unable to stop the hunger and frantic search to gratify one's sensual desires, one gets exhausted by many ingenious schemes and clandestine activities. As a result mindfulness slackens and one finds the mind at the mercy of Māra's fifth army, lethargy and sleepiness.

This army is completely overcome only in a fully enlightened person. Nevertheless, as the factors of enlightenment are developed, one dispenses with more and more sleep. In fact, at the insight stage of rise and fall, one is boosted up with energy. This energy can go on by itself. One becomes accomplished in energy as the mind is crystal clear, fresh and alert. We are told in the Anguttara Nikāya that Moggallāna encountered sloth and torpor while striving for the higher stages of enlightenment. The Buddha gave some pointers and a strategy to combat this fifth army of Māra.

a. Sleepiness is aggravated by thoughts that encourage rest or taking a nap. One should therefore make a firm *resolution* to put away such lazy thoughts at once and strive on with vigour. One can also choose to *increase the number of objects* to watch. For example, if there is an interval between the rising and the falling of the abdomen, it can be filled in with other notings, for instance of the sitting posture or of various touch points. The second method can be illustrated with a simile. There is a bright child in the class who finds the work easy and gets bored. His boredom can be challenged with an increase in his work load.

b. The characteristic of sloth and torpor is a shrunken state which does not pick up objects easily. The opposite is *accurate application* of the mind on the object. For example one makes the mind note precisely each rise and fall. This has the power to open and refresh the mind.

c. In the advice to Moggallāna, the Buddha recommended the *recitation* of inspiring passages. But care should be taken that this does not disturb the other yogis.

d. The *mental recollection* of inspiring passages of the Dhamma is also invigorating.

e. *Pulling* the ear lobes, *rubbing* the body, head and limbs vigorously helps to stimulate the blood circulation and thus clears up drowsiness.

f. One may also *wash* or *splash* the face with cold water and then look mindfully in all directions, for example at the sky full of stars.

g. One may also *visualize light*, the moon, stars, etc., or actually sit in a lighted room. Another interpretation of this perception of light is the creation of an intense wish to see more clearly what one is actually doing.

h. If all the above six methods fail, then one can get up to do *brisk walking*. But bear in mind that while doing so, one has to be very mindful and restrained in the senses, while trying to keep the mind concentrated on the process of walking.

i. If this still does not work, then it is time for a *graceful surrender*. That is, go to bed mindfully, lying down in "the lion's posture."[5] Before sleeping, set the alarm—not of the clock but in the mind—and then continue to watch the rising and falling processes of the abdomen. At the very moment of waking up, be mindful. A very short nap is allowable in the case of sleepiness due to a heavy meal. But this should not be longer than the time it takes for the hair of a monk to dry!

Mara's sixth army is ***fear***. It can arise in the meditator who lives in the forest and deter him in the practice. Sounds which may lead to images of non-existent ghosts or wild beasts can produce fear. In meditation centres in the city these sorts of incidents may not be so obvious. But this sixth army of Māra can assume the form of dread of interviews, disappointment, inferiority complex, self-pity, and all sorts of paranoia. If we are able to transcend all these, we will have a lot of inspirations instead.

5. The lion's posture is the Buddha's way to rest, lying on the right side and sustaining the head with the right arm.

The seventh army is ***doubt***. A yogi may begin to doubt the authenticity of others' reports, one's own capability *(maybe I don't have enough pāramīs ...*) and the method of practice (*this method is great for others but maybe it doesn't suit me ...*), the teacher (*even during the Buddha's time different people had affinities with different teachers ...*), and so on. Doubt is yet another formidable army of Māra.

The eighth army is ***conceit***. When the practice becomes better one may have many unusual experiences. As a result one may feel that one has attained to some supernormal state. When assaulted by this subversive force of Māra, one is not willing to listen to the teacher's instructions and may begin to look down on other peoples' practice or other traditions. One may even end up being a fanatic.

The ninth army comes in the form of ***gains, fame,*** and ***reverence*** as a result of good practice. One can easily become attached to all these, thus slackening in one's own practice. This is comparable to the rare flowers of a bamboo that spell the end of the plant.

Māra's tenth and last army can arise out of the respect and homage shown by people, which tempt the yogi to greatly ***overestimate*** and ***exalt*** himself or herself while ***disparaging*** others.

The yogi who cannot defeat the armies of Māra is like a titan who lacks courageous effort. One who has the ability to win each and every battle is indeed endowed with heroic effort. There are three phases of heroic effort, the *launching phase* whereby the initial effort is made, the *booster phase* when increased effort is required to overcome the assault by hindrances, pain, and so forth, and the *sustaining phase* when practice is good. In the last phase one still has to keep looking out for infiltration by subversive elements from Māra's armies like pride, complacency, fame, gains, veneration, etc., and clear them up. The energy needed for this clearing up operation comes from the touchdown phase that leads to final victory in the war with Māra. At this stage one must still remind oneself that the end of the journey is not yet reached.

As there are enemies within and without, so wars are fought internally and externally. The external wars should be avoided at all instances. They cause immense suffering and senseless destruction. But the energetic and mindful resistance to the mental corruptions is a cause of much peace and happiness. Weapons of war are lethal but are also subject to wear and tear with continued use. In the days of old, for instance, the more heads were cut off, the blunter the warrior's sword became.

The weapons employed in the war with Māra's armed forces, however, are not only effective, formidable, and powerful, but increase in efficiency and sharpness with frequent usage. For example, the more continuously mindfulness is used, the sharper it becomes, enabling wisdom to penetrate into even more profound depths of reality. With the deepening of practice heroic effort is strengthened, as the spiritual weapons are incredibly sharpened, until one cuts through all delusion with a single stroke and attains enlightenment.

CHAPTER SIX

Nibbāna

Nibbāna is said to be a reality just like consciousness, mental factors, and matter. It is therefore not a mere concept or imagination. It is also a mistaken view that the Noble Ones have a special mind-body complex or a special core to the mind-body complex. It is, however, true that Nibbāna cannot be really described to one who has not realized it. One description is *freedom from all suffering,* that is, *peace.* It is something better than all the good things in life. The Dhamma classifies happiness as of two kinds, happiness *associated with feelings* (like pleasure) and happiness *dissociated from feelings,* which refers to the peace of Nibbāna. The first kind of happiness is *conditioned* by three factors: the base, the object, and consciousness. The second kind of happiness is Nibbāna which is *unconditioned.*

The first kind of happiness, sensual pleasure, lasts a short time but one has to work hard to get it. One can also get sick of sense pleasures. In the search for them, one encounters a lot of suffering. In the final analysis these sense pleasures are impermanent, troublesome, and illusory.

For ordinary folks, happiness is bound up with feelings. They cannot think of it dissociated from feelings. So their satisfaction in life is sensual pleasures because they can't think of it otherwise. To illustrate that there can be a happiness which is not associated with sensual pleasure, we take the example of a millionaire who can enjoy many things like food, music, etc. After enjoying sensual pleasures he goes to bed and sleeps so soundly that he does not want to wake up.

When someone does indeed wake him up, so that he is able to enjoy all the blissful pleasures of the senses again, he gets angry. Why? Because that sleep, though not directly a sensual pleasure, is a kind of happiness.

Suffering in this world originates from the defilements. In order to overcome suffering, to get nibbānic peace, we have to remove the cause. Therefore yogis practise mindfulness, which guards against the defilements arising from moment to moment at the six sense doors. When they do so they are at least temporarily released and have peace. But if one is vigilant and persistent one can reach the peace that is timeless!